HOW TO READ A COMIC BOOK

Comic books are made up of pictures in boxes, called panels. Look at each of these panels from left to right, and top to bottom.

Read the speech bubbles, caption boxes and any sound effects from left to right, too. Together with the images, these will tell you the story.

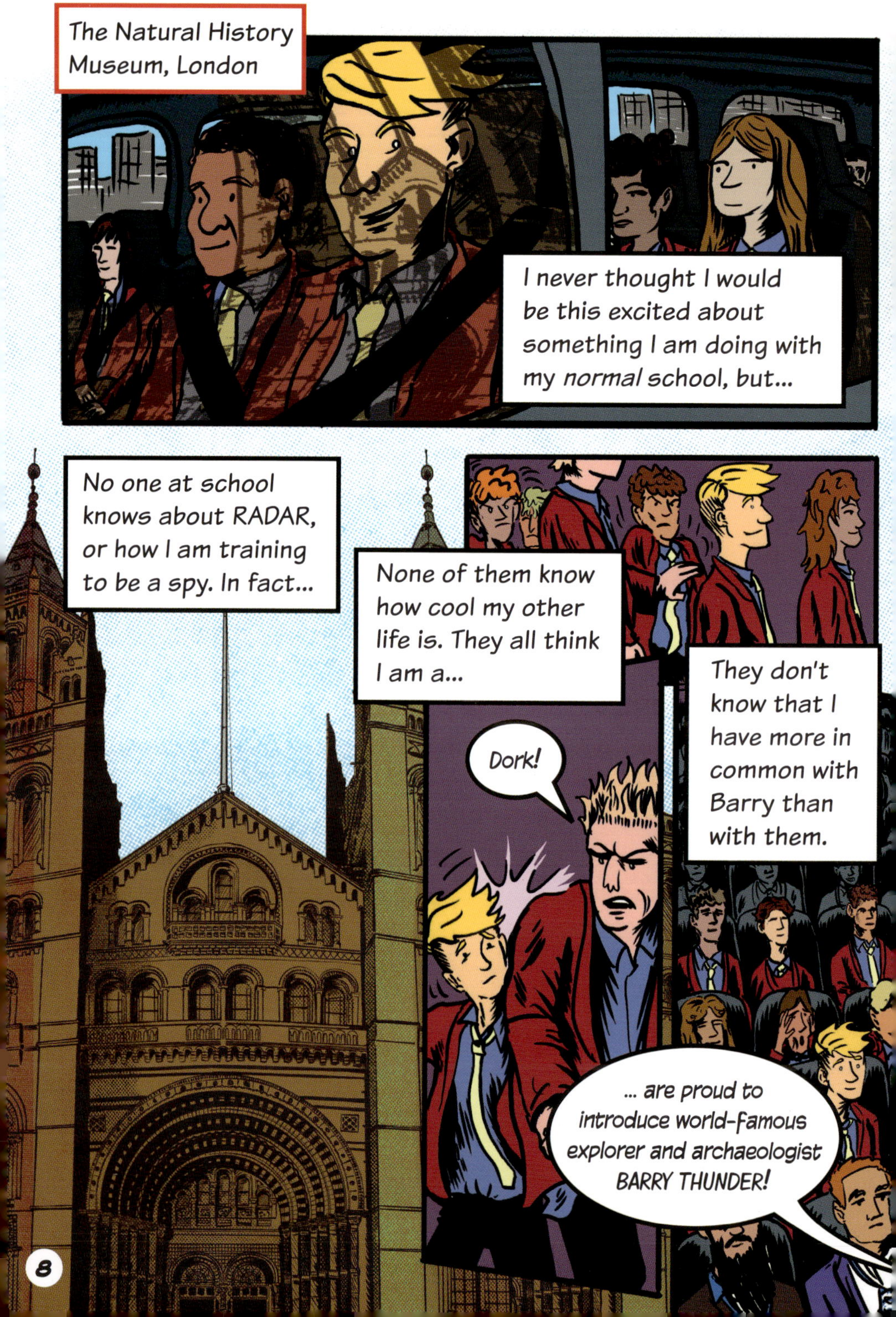

... for us to disappear into the shadows.

Chase, I know it's you. Come out and no one need be hurt.

This way. Stay low.

Fat chance.

Hi, I am Nathan.

Barry Thunder.

Er, um, I guess... I wasn't expecting to have a fight today.

I know. I'm a big fan. What happened out there? I thought you had three black belts.

They were real. But like you, Barry, they were not what they said they were. They were...

... aliens!

These ancient aliens gave us technology...

... into something amazing.

They visited...

... all the great civilisations...

Something that has since been lost.

... of the ancient world.

... that transformed our ancestors' world...

But what was once lost has now been found.

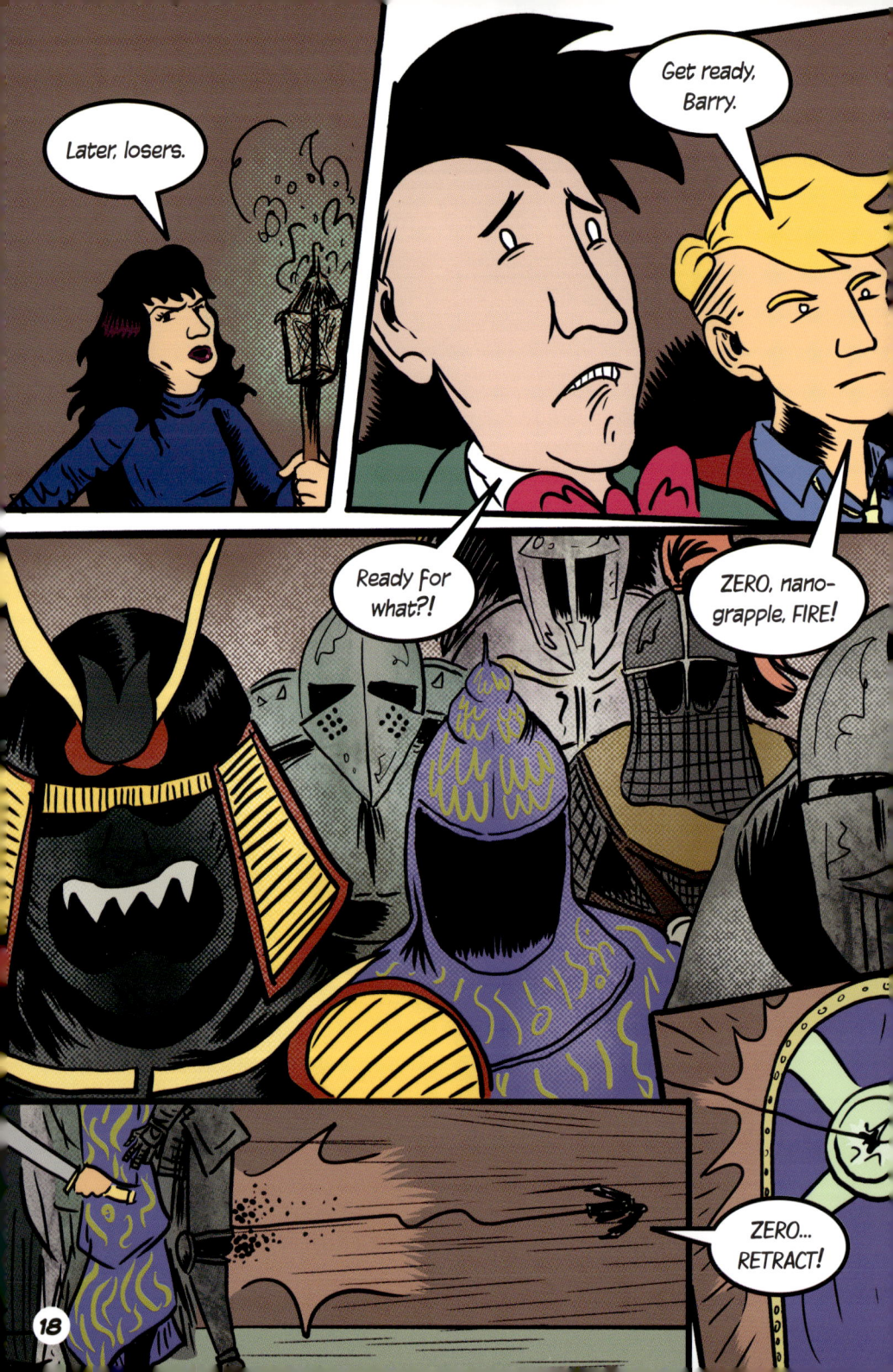

There was no way I could leave Barry here while I went after Zara.

I mean, just look at him!

@2024 BookLife Publishing Ltd.
King's Lynn, Norfolk, PE30 4LS, UK

ISBN 978-1-80505-285-2

All rights reserved. Printed in India.
A catalogue record for this book is available from the British Library.

The Chase Files: History Chase
Written by Robin Twiddy
Illustrated by Kel Winser

ABOUT BOOKLIFE GRAPHIC READERS

BookLife Graphic Readers are designed to encourage reluctant readers to take the next step in their reading adventure. These books are a perfect accompaniment to the BookLife Readers phonics scheme and are designed to be read by children who have a good grasp on reading but are reluctant to pick up a full-prose book. Graphic Readers combine graphic and prose storytelling in a way that aids comprehension and presents a more accessible reading experience for reluctant readers and lovers of comic books.

ABOUT THE AUTHOR

Robin is a lifelong comic book fan whose love for the medium led to it being the topic of his undergraduate dissertation. He is the author of many great BookLife titles, including several entries into the BookLife phonic reader scheme. Robin loves action, adventure and humour and brings these elements together into exciting narratives you won't forget.

ABOUT THE ILLUSTRATOR

Kel has been drawing cartoons, superheroes and comics for as long as he can remember. He divides his time between teaching the next generation of cartoonists, making illustrations and comics for himself and publishers, spending time with his family, and growing an enormous beard! Kel lives in Norwich UK, with his wife and son.